And the Stones Fell Open

A Leeds Poetry Anthology

© Copyright the authors 2020
Published by Yaffle Press, 2020

https://www.yafflepress.co.uk/

All rights reserved. No part of this book may be copied, reproduced, stored in a retrieval system or transmitted, in any form or by any electronic or mechanical means without the prior permission of the copyright holder.

ISBN: 978-1-913122-11-9

Cover design: Lorna Faye Dunsire

Cover photo: Mark Connors

Typesetting: Mike Farren

Editor: Ian Harker

Acknowledgements

'The shock troops of the revolution' by Merv Lebor appeared in *Any Change: Poetry in a Hostile Environment*, edited by Ian Duhig.

'Did you dream of fire' by Joe Williams appeared on *I am not a silent poet*, edited by Reuben Woolley, in April 2018. Reuben passed away in December 2019, and Joe Williams and the editor would like to dedicate this poem to Reuben and his tireless hard work for poetry, the results of which reached across the world.

'Morality tale' by Becky Cherriman appeared on the *Celebrating Change* website in October 2019. https://celebratingchange.blog/

'Three navigators, 1846' by Matthew Hedley Stoppard was commissioned by Otley Town Council and a recording of it features on the DVD 'The Navvies Who Built The Bramhope Tunnel' made by Catapult Films.

'Las locas' by Lydia Kennaway appeared in *A History of Walking* (Happen*Stance* Press, 2019).

'Songs of Praise' by Carole Bromley was published in *Well Versed* (The Morning Star).

'Present' by Emma Storr was written for the charity Growing Points https://growingpoints.co.uk

'TV haibun' by Rachel Bower appeared in *Stand* magazine 17.2 (2019).

'Invisible injuries' by Sandra Burnett was written as part of Chapel FM's #LD50 project, celebrating fifty years since the twining of the cities of Dortmund and Leeds, and subsequently appeared in Sandra's collection *Between Sea and Sky*, published by Half Moon Books.

'Thomas Piketty picks his way through the shattered shopfronts' by Ian Harker appeared in *Rules of Survival*, Templar Poetry, 2017.

Preface

We are not quite sure what the poet Wallace Stevens meant when he said that people ought to like poetry the way children like the snow. I've always thought that he was pointing to the way that poetry, like snow, can help us see a landscape through fresh eyes. It is an adventure to go out into the snow but it can be startling in its icy reality and we have to re-navigate our route, but, at the same time, it allows us see our own breath in the unforgiving lower temperature. Poetry works in the same way; and here we have a good example.

This brilliant anthology is a celebration of Leeds, its cityscape, its people, its problems and potential, its shadow and its light. It helps us see with a better clarity but also reminds us that our work is to constantly reimagine our locality and our place and behaviour in it. Poetry's subversion is that it can present a sub-version, an imagined and distilled reality beneath our falsities and distractions. Poems invite us to this place and invite us to live within its clarified landscape of depth. In their unique ways the poems here do this and consequently construct a vision for the city that helps us be truthful about what is but hopeful and unapologetic about what may yet be. Poetry makes music out of noise and here the complexity of the city of Leeds is captured in what Les Murray called the 'wholespeak' of poetry rather than the 'narrowspeak' of so much contemporary communication. We need today politics with renewed vision and spirituality with greater political commitment. This collection shows us the way.

It was a privilege to give the Hook Lecture in 2019 and to encourage us all to see the urgency and vitality of poetry, the prophetic and protest in a world that is snoring itself into danger. Reading these poems moved me greatly as I saw all three of these vocations in full flow. I loved them as I love the snow.

Mark Oakley, Dean of St John's College, Cambridge

Contents

An Aroko for David Oluwale	Ian Duhig	1
Industry of unemployment	Lence	2
The shock troops of the Revolution	Merv Lebor	3
When the last man closed his eyes	Andy Armitage	4
Elijah	Aziz Dixon	5
Treasure	Rachel Flint	6
Neighbourhood library	Abdullah Adekola	7
Branding protest	Hannah Stone	9
Darryl broke the 4th wall	Lisa Boardman	10
Job seeker	William Thirsk-Gaskill	12
Did you dream of fire?	Joe Williams	14
Choose your tribe	Joe Williams	15
It takes a village	Adrian Salmon	17
Mistaken	Adrian Salmon	18
Rosa Brigante	Su Ryder	20
Morality tale	Becky Cherriman	22
Black walking	Jason Allen Paisant	24
Dorothy Wilkinson, suffragette	Richard Wilcocks	26
I'm just in it for the parking	Malcolm Henshall	28
Bruises beneath feathers	Matthew Hedley Stoppard	30
Three navigators, 1846	Matthew Hedley Stoppard	32
Las locas	Lydia Kennaway	34
Songs of Praise	Carole Bromley	36
Flitin'	Carole Bromley	37
Present	Emma Storr	38
Resurrection	Eileen Neil	39
Coral made	Rachel Bower	40
TV haibun	Rachel Bower	41
Scenes from a Cold War Childhood	Oz Hardwick	42
Desperate for a seat	Cath Nichols	43
Why I don't like Wednesdays	Cath Nichols	45

Invisible injuries	*Sandra Burnett*	47
"B comes to stay at my place"	*Ann Wong*	48
In which god appears as a busker	*Kristina Diprose*	49
The Truth Project	*Jane Kite*	50
Stonewall	*Jack Mac*	51
Madness	*Moira Garland*	53
The outsiders	*Becky Howcroft*	54
Heretic	*Anna Sutcliffe*	56
Thomas Piketty picks his way through the shattered shopfronts	*Ian Harker*	57
Come the Revolution	*Testament*	59

An Aroko for David Oluwale

Oluwale is Yoruba for *'God Has Come Home'*
but he came to find Hell in God's Own Country,
no home but cold Leeds streets or police cells,
in his asylum only electroconvulsive therapy.

Now by the Aire, where David drowned fleeing
policemen's boots, his feet light from hunger,
my small nomadic cowrie garden grows for one
who'd grown to be a shell of himself in this city.

An empty cowrie is full as an egg with meanings:
Gods' eyes, they make *arokos*, magic messages.
Because *efa*, Yoruba for six, has the same letters
as the word to draw, my six cowries set down here

draw David's Christian ghost into Oshun's arms,
water Goddess with a name of water, that he too
might step into the true meaning of his own name
borne back to Africa where the river of us all rose.

This alchemy of cold fire on the Aire's earth makes
nothing happen, like poetry, yet makes something
from nothing for a man treated like he was nothing,
making room to reflect on river water running softly.

Ian Duhig

Industry of unemployment

As the doors are unlocked
And the queue outside gets moving,
And we're filtered into appointments
Seeking employments quite confusing
What websites are we using?
They keep asking us that!
We're just watching the words we're choosing,
When we have to answer back
Signing up to these different sites,
But they all wanna know our details,
It's a constant flow of emails!
If the coach is pushing a job on you,
There's no getting away!
They'll say you've got to attend the assessment day
Still we don't get paid,
They send us away with the same old cold response
We're here to get you a job they said,
Just not the role you want
So we keep on top of that job search
Filling out every space,
And we hand it over the desk,
Then we sit there and we wait
And whilst we do we're looking around the room
Just wishing that we weren't there
The security guards wish they weren't either
But they just seem to stare,
It's a place where the interviews just lead to another
We'll be lucky if they need us for cover
Still trying to be the change if the universe will let it,
Because this is creativity on universal credit

Lence

The shock troops of the revolution

The blood of the fuzz bulleted on the road,
Injured in the class war...
The sun's too hot for shooting-up
I, too old to see my life spasm out of control
Yet again.
I was the revolution.
We'd been told to kill.

In 'youff' I strapped a cocktail to my chest
For oppression had scored the inner city,
Raised in red-glazed tenements,
Blocked flats, lacking all warmth.
A selfish, selfless flame,
I threw bottles of meths.
I was the revolution,
Drunk on lust that was recharged in hatred
For men who minted paradise
On our folk's sun-stroked backs
And women, labouring
A dying city's wearied spirit.

Now I'm left walking at the side
Of a scorched road,
Age-old rage momentarily calm,
Cleansed of killing...
'You are the shock-troops of the revolution',
I was told.
I believed.
I felt exploited, hollow,
Like oppression had won,
Yet the revolution was still
Like an ever-widening chasm
In my heart.

Merv Lebor

When the last man closed his eyes

and everything he had seen
was forgotten
and all of his dreams and his sweat
led to nothing
and the skies darkened
and the houses gaped
in the wind
and the oceans filled the streets
and the stones fell open
plastic went on being plastic

Andy Armitage

Elijah

Hang your consonants on a washing line,
it's the vowels that count. Articulate clearly for me,
presto ma non troppo,
red lorry, yellow lorry, lavender lorry.
Unless you listen to each other,
unless you watch me, there will be
drought and famine, flood, earthquake and fire:
it will not go well for you.

The prophet has come to this rural idyll.
The sign is in the hall –
Yorkshire's best kept village; all the passion
of junior football outside the window,
and, at noon, a wedding across the road.
A buzzard is mewing, above the sunlit moors.

Elijah lived in a harsh landscape,
had a hard time of it. 'In opposition
to the whole world,' the composer reported
(having met him), 'yet borne
on angels' wings.'
Where in me
is the voice of Baal,
the prophet's reply?

Become this music, the drama, live
the passion, in the moment, on the beat,
and please,   ...watch me.

Know this also: after the fire
a still small voice, and in that voice,
as in the music, was the Lord.

Aziz Dixon

Treasure
For Guilia and Roberta

There is no room for nervousness
When meeting your support worker.
    They see your nakedness,
    The bed hair, dirty underwear, duvet days.
Unfiltered life.
    The part that's usually behind closed doors.

    Kindness is gold, dignity sacred.
    My treasure is found in gentle Sicilian voices
    'Morning carina, how did you sleep?'
    Instant sunlight enters the room
    Makes it home, makes it human.

Leeds has welcomed them,
Given them opportunities, love and acceptance.
Though they long for loquats,
They wouldn't be anywhere else.
Only when the Bre*it word is mentioned
Does a cloud cross their faces.

Rachel Flint

Neighbourhood Library

Compton Road Library in Harehills Leeds
A cold old building even in summer
Abdulaziz and Alya came with me
By foot or bike we had to go
Overstayed in the library and in Leeds
More community spaces needed
Fun and freedom is welcome
Fables, Truths and well-spent youth
Books and comics by the bag load
Had to pay a few fines
Reading and scheming all summer
Everything goes on your record
Claiming our prize of seeds and stickers
On the PC playing games, dial up internet days
Doom, Asterix, Habbo Hotel
GTA and some Minecraft
In the early days of Youtube
Artemis Fowl, Alex Rider
Fun and games on the Gameboy
Only a few had MP3s
Noughts and crosses thanks to Malorie
From Summer days
To Northern nights at the Northern Lights
In a daemon daze
With boys that smile and boys that cry
Boys who took and boys who give
Boys who ran and boys who hid
I've always liked the boy who lived
I've always liked the boy in the striped pyjamas
From Leeds to Lagos, Kingston to Dortmund
People need hope, we need stories
We need each other, we need kindness
I'm trying to stay black and stay human
I'm trying to keep my sanity, serve humanity

Submit to Allah and stay free
It's a good day to be alive
Now as good a time as any
A better world is possible
Maybe she's on her way
Take nothing for granted
Take nothing as given
Tomorrow is for those
Who prepare today.

Abdullah Adekola

Branding protest
(Note: words in italics come from FATFACE's marketing straplines:
We proudly make clothes that reflect the happy healthy lifestyles of our customers.)

Here's a brand for the rest of us,
the anxious and the insecure;
for those of us not feeling great,
who smoke too much, grow cellulite,
who, frankly, couldn't give a toss
if what we hang up on the rail
are *hero pieces* or just clothes;
for those of us whose *built to last*
are garments worn for decades, patched
and mended, make-do as our lives,
threadbare as false hope but cosy.
A brand for those whose *big hearts* find
friends in those who feel forgotten,
those folk whose Facebook statuses
don't tend to gather many 'likes.'

Let's rebrand life *work in progress*;
its *focus* – accepting yourself,
objective – giving half a shit
about some things that really count.
So shrug on your shabby old shirt,
smile at strangers at the bus stop,
choose green energy, dig a well,
sign that petition, plant a tree.
Above all, cast your vote.
Let's rebrand homo sapiens
'human beings, humans doing.'

Hannah Stone

Darryl broke the 4th wall

Darryl broke the 4th wall
Between reality and the unknown
In a park surrounded by pigeon scum

Where I lay on my jacket legs outstretched
He loitered in the vicinity
And I accidentally caught his eye
As he mumbled objections to the pigeons
That flapped aimlessly around him

And so he punctured his way into my world
With attacks of small talk and introductions
And fires raged in my skull
And my obligated tongue ached
As it butchered its way through mundane
Questions and answers

He was young
A college student
He smoked cigars inhaling pointedly
Inviting me wordlessly to comment

But when the first break of inevitable silence came
He took another deep drag
Turned to me and said
'Excuse me but I think I need to break the 4th wall'

And he took himself off
A few feet away
Where he began his monologue to camera
Staring through the constraints of
Accepted realism

I watched the changing expressions on his face as
He changed the inflection in his speech
Engaging an unseen audience

I was half an episode worth of material
In series one of his life

I thought of all the times I had unconsciously searched for my
	audience
The audience knows you
Loves you

To break the 4th wall
Is to try and talk to god

And Darryl
As it turned out
Had it sussed

Lisa Boardman

Job seeker

The week after I was made redundant, I applied for a job as Director of Strategy with Paradise Futures plc. The remuneration package included a chauffeur-driven limousine, generous pension, comprehensive private healthcare, requirement only to attend 12 half-day meetings per year, stock purchase scheme, and a salary of 100,000 US dollars per annum, paid via a shell company registered in Qatar, and transferred to the UK via a double Dutch sandwich. Application was by recommendation from recognised agents and intermediaries, only.

The month after I was made redundant, I applied for a job as Information Governance Lead with Warm Fuzzy Feelings Incorporated. The remuneration package included a car allowance of £350 per month, pension, subsidised private healthcare, 35 days holiday, performance bonus, and a salary of £65,000 per annum. Application was by CV and covering letter.

Three months after I was made redundant, I applied for a job as business analyst with Expectations Limited. The reward package included 21 days holiday after 6 complete months of service, a salary of £23,000, subsidised staff canteen, and access to the games room on alternate Wednesdays and Fridays. Application was made after a 3-hour wait in an unheated room full of plastic chairs.

Six months after I was made redundant, I applied for a job as junior technician with Scientific Clipboards. The terms and conditions included payment of £6.70 per full hour worked, free access to the first aid box, the eye wash station, and the anti-cyanide kit, and twice-yearly visits from a mobile shop selling discounted shoes with steel toe-protectors. Application was made after being told to report to a different office four times, and then completing an assault course based on one used by the Royal Marines.

Eleven Months after I was made redundant, I applied for a job as ash-pit scraper with Experimental Subjects Kommanditgesellschaft. The terms and conditions included non-transferable and non-exchangeable plastic tokens, providing discretionary access to water, oxygen, nutrients, and sunlight on alternate solstices. Application was made after crawling through a maze of concrete pipes filled with raw sewage.

An unspecified period after I was made redundant, I applied to be set free of earthly wants, no longer to be exploited, judged, monitored, and assessed. Application was by means of regular exercise, meditation, prayer, and fasting.

I didn't get it.

William Thirsk-Gaskill

Did you dream of fire?
In memory of Reuben Woolley

Fire in the desert.
Fire in the streets.
Fire that tore through the air at night.
Fire in the bellies of those
who are not with you,
so must be against you.
Fire that burnt through your bed.

Did you wake up screaming?
Did you dream of blood?

Joe Williams

Choose your tribe

Roundhead or Cavalier
Guardian or Telegraph
Sacred or secular
Republican or Democrat
Rachel or Phoebe
Slytherin or Gryffindor
Zeno or Epicurus
Spectrum or Commodore

Choose your tribe

Windows or Apple
United or City
Lager or bitter
Tupac or Biggie
Tesco or Waitrose
Arsenal or Spurs
Beano or Dandy
Oasis or Blur

In or out
Choose your tribe

Mod or rocker
Punk or prog
Tea or coffee
Cat or dog
League or union
Friend or foe
Sith or Jedi
Yes or no

Choose your tribe

Spice Girls or All Saints
Montague or Capulet
Marlboro or Silk Cut
Seb Coe or Steve Ovett
Playboy or Penthouse
Marvel or DC
Grandad or Uncle Albert
Cowgirl or missionary

With us or against us
Choose your tribe

Joe Williams

It takes a village

It takes a village, we've always said,
half meaning it, half not. But it takes a village
so there'll be one to notice; a village
so there'll be one to love, one to teach; a village
so there'll be one to stand up in defence.

And now maybe it takes a city, a country, or a world
to say *you don't go down today, not on my watch*,
to throw open the cages, to plunge into the cold dark
like a boar rooting, seeking that precious smell:
of childhood, possibility, and hope.

Hooyah! we say to those who cage you,
Hooyah! to those who hold you down.
It takes a village to raise you,
it takes a city, a country, and a world.
And we're yours.

(Written in response to the rescue of the Thai 'Wild Boars' junior football team in the Tham Luang caves, and reports of immigrant children detained by ICE in the US, June/July 2018. The Thai Marines tweeted 'Hooyah!' each time a child was brought up safe.)

Adrian Salmon

Mistaken

Mom, this is so exciting, it will change everything,
it is a new story, mom, you'll see.
It will be so much better.

Mom, it is not going to be comfortable
but it will be worth it. It will be
only for a little, and then I will write to you.

Mom, there are so many of us,
we do not know each other,
we do not trust those who will take us.

Mom, it is dark, we mustn't make noise.
We do not know where we are going,
it is cold – it never stops,

the cold and the noise
and the smell and the cold –
I try just to think of you.

Mom, the noises are changing:
every hour there is less breathing,
every hour there is more silence.

Mom, it is so cold – I do not want to think
about what is happening. Mom,
I did not think this could happen.

Mom, I have been mistaken
about this story. I have been
mistaken.

Mom, I love you so much.
Mom I am dying
because I cannot breathe.

(In memory of those found in the Essex lorry trailer, October 2019)

Adrian Salmon

Rosa Brigante

The seed of Rosa Brigante
cracked the core of the Earth in its cradle.
Shoots burrowed to crack the virgin crust,
suckling iron from the mantle.
Her rootstock was a tight fist,
and her tongue honed to a thorn.
Her spreading petals were the hue
of battle-stripped skull and bone.

She split a seam at Lagentium,
bled Spittal Hardwick Lane.
Ermine Street was her vestment,
anthracite her Sceptre and Orb.
The mother of Cartimandua,
her sisters and her daughter,
came to wash her sword in the river Aire,
to rinse her shield in the Calder.

Some hag who called herself Iron,
tried to undermine her by starvation,
knocked the bottle out of the babby's mouth,
no more hope, no more Ledston Luck.
But thirty-five years after –
with Ferrybridge falling to dust –
the fruit of Rosa Brigante's hip
stands defiant, all bloodstains and rust.

And she'll bloom on, the flower of the coalfields,
guttural, beautiful rage,
defender of the colloquial truth,
feral in petal and claw,
Rosa Brigante Alba
ledgers this world's defaults in lost lives,
whether quick, dead, still born or miscarried,
the children of miners' wives.

Su Ryder

Morality tale

Picture every one of the world's weapons as part of a colossal web.
Barrel bombs. Recoilless guns. Rockets. Anti-aircraft missiles.
    Mines. Sarin.

Trace them from where they end up amid
voluptuous hills and ravaged cities,
    green fields and passes,

ruptured bodies and people breathing blood instead of air
to the man (for it is usually a man) with the rocket on his shoulder,
    finger on the enter button.

Pursue him to the one who gave the order
and he who gave him his —
    puppetry, the profit of the puppeteer.

Let him dangle in the tremoring tangle of triumphalism
and what it will warp to in the long nights of his life:
    slow death venom.

Trail their route — stolen from government forces
when battles are won, stacked in national air force planes,
    commercial flights or smuggled in lorries.

Stop off — Iran, Qatar, Iraq, Saudi, Turkey
(who keep some to themselves to settle old scores).
    Humans like to stockpile

what they haven't exploited of war,
wind tight fractured limbs and caught hearts;
    secret airlift

from the former Yugoslavia where the tears of a hundred eyes
spring from the forests, where once ancient bridges
    are now nothing but stone

to where a woman jokes on an assembly line,
a man releases
    a substance into test-tubes.

Feel along that viscid twine:
steel and fire
      to base metal

to funding. High street banks
and stocks and shares.
      Pensions —

us dining out our retirements
on spider morality tales we refuse to hear, Arachnes hanging
      on twitching threads.

Becky Cherriman

Black walking
(A found poem)[1]

In the mist I see
long lines of blacks walking
death walks to slave ships
black footprints
on cathedrals and monuments
of the city

I dream black immigrant feet
my family on the move working
second, third and fourth jobs

Is that why
   hiking feels so strange us
   walking without purpose
   going up then down
   arriving at the same spot

Or maybe there is
a purpose   something
to find in the peaks

people who came here
long before
whose stories are in the land
they claim isn't yours

---

[1] Based on the words of Testament, as reported in Bridget Minamore, 'Black Men Walking: A hilly hike through 500 years of Black British History', The Guardian, 23 January 2018.
https://www.theguardian.com/stage/2018/jan/23/black-men-walking-royal-exchange-manchester-testament

Is walking a reclamation
a moving slowly enough to say
this is a land you can take your time with

these peaks are safe   I won't need to run

Jason Allen Paisant

Dorothy Wilkinson, suffragette

You should have heard me sing that song
in German, me the fair maiden - before it started.
Pianist father, Prussian mother picking holes,
dreaming they were both still studying
music at the Berlin Conservatorium.
Love. *Ein Traum*. Copied it out - nectar.
Ich hielt dich fest. I held you tight
and now no more will let you go.
The poet wrote that - well-worn, I know.

You should have heard me banging that
suffrage drum, swinging up Woodhouse Lane
to thousands protesting on the moor.
Doing my bit for the cause - before it started.
Our anthem *March of the Women*.
And Leonora? Harmonised with her
but my heart flinched when she told me
of her plan to smash the crown jewels
with an iron bar – for me, a stride too far.

You should have seen me waltzing
with Clifford beneath patriotic bunting.
Army surgeon, held me tight, me a half-Hun,
lured on by uniforms and love – it started.
Remember that preacher's sermon about
the Hun wanting to scourge us with scorpions?
Clifford didn't vote for that, carried my photo
to a Casualty Clearing Station near Ypres.
Fitted out for most tasks – but nil gas masks.

I know you watched me weeping at
his burial in Lawnswood. Brought back
quivering with shell-shock, rallied a while,
then asphyxiated by Spanish flu. His lungs
filled with blood. Staunched my pain, voted

to volunteer as nurse, not just routine duties
but compering ward parties, playing piano,
scorning those rules on avoiding intimacy,
and comforting wounded men, including you,
Alfred, *Liebling, mein Mann*. Let's sing.

Richard Wilcocks

I'm just in it for the parking

I am a man
I am a man

I am a man born of a woman who was fit and healthy
I am a man born of a woman who had an unseen virus

I am a man whose father worked in a shop
I am a man whose father worked in a factory

I am a man whose birth brought pleasure to my parents
I am a man whose birth brought pleasure to my parents but also pain

I am a man who grew as most men grow
I am a man whose growth took a different path

When I was five, I went to the local school
When I was five, I travelled 10 miles to school

I walked to school
I went in a van

I played football
I cannot walk, I use a wheelchair

I am ordinary
Apparently, I am special

My parents made me feel special
My experiences made me feel anything but special

I went to University and gained my degree
I went to a 'Centre'.

I go to the local pub
I can't get into the local pub

I am a teacher
I cannot talk

I have trouble finding a parking spot
That's no problem for the driver of my van

I am thirty, married with children
I am thirty and still live with my parents

I look after my children
My parents look after me.

I will live long and see my children married
I may live long and see my parents die

My children will see I'm alright as I grow old
What will I do when my parent's die?

Malcolm Henshall

Bruises beneath feathers

Heavy clouds overhead
cast moving shadows
like a stranger walking
past your bedroom door.
Drying rain tightens skin
near Clarence Dock;
you tug the children back
from the railings,
then let down your umbrella
and use it to skewer a seagull.

You complain of seeing
every hour after midnight
carrying sickly children
around Temple Newsam Farm.
No lambs or piglets
to stop the tantrums and help
piece together broken sleep.
They call it straw,
you call it scarecrow guts
holding a pheasant in a headlock.

Marshalling the picnic blanket
proves too difficult amidst
quacking and rumble of Otley pedalos.
You push the children towards
the playground, a swan waddles up
from the Wharfe, and your eyes
meet as you wring its slender neck.

There will be no one to stroke
your hand when the city's statues
are spotless and the sky is empty.
No one to hear you say sorry,
with your last breath,

for the pigeonless parks and squares,
and the canal and Aire
bereft of mallards.

Matthew Hedley Stoppard

Three navigators, 1846

The price of wheat had risen two shillings
and the temperature had dropped in January
like the first workman to die that year; falling 100 feet
in shaft No. 14, ascending by rope and bucket
after he had prepared a blast at the bottom
to lengthen Bramhope tunnel and open the earth.

But why should a man lower himself deep in the earth
for the reward of a purse full of shillings?
His top would've been blown from his bottom
if he had not landed on the lit fuse that January
with his remains shovelled up and collected in a bucket
rather than properly buried at 6 feet.

Another was slain by a fragment falling 70 feet;
a teenager, not 20 years on this Earth,
struck on the temple by a small stone from the bucket
perhaps the size of an acorn or a shilling.
He died like his comrade back in January
only this one was dragged up from the bottom

to take the air and recover, bottom
lip wobbling, unsteady on his feet.
A chill crept into his bones, cold as January,
sleeping outside on the damp earth;
the doctor covered his eyes with two shillings
a fortnight after that blunder beneath the bucket.

For the third, injustice came by the bucket-
load. Some would've left him to rot at the bottom
of the cutting and not stump up the shillings
to bury him in Pool with roses at his feet.
Crushed by falling rocks, unwelcome in the earth,
too – unwelcome as Christmas gifts in January.

For three days, solace remained barren as January
and still no flowers were gathered in buckets.

Finally, they found a resting place in holy earth
at Otley Parish Church, the coffin lowered to the bottom
of a grave respectfully dug, the whole 6 feet –
for some, peace takes pride over pennies and shillings.

For every person as hard and cold as earth in January,
there are tenfold who don't care for shillings; their kindness a bucket
with no bottom, steadfast to help the fallen to their feet.

Matthew Hedley Stoppard

Las locas
(from *A History of Walking*
For the Mothers of the Disappeared, Buenos Aires, 1977 - 2006)

Standing or sitting is forbidden.
So we walk. Every week,
we walk in the Plaza in circles.
Week after week, year after year.
They call us The Madwomen.
We'd all heard whispers
about The Disappeared.
Just having those words
in your ear was poison.
This is my daughter, Maria.
She is beautiful, even
in black and white. Her smile
is now five years old.
A strong woman,
a grown woman, I know,
but always and ever my child.
She came to me with flowers
for my birthday. Next morning,
she was not at work.
Nor the day after that.
Nor the day after that.
They call us The Madwomen.
We wear white headscarves.
Mine is embroidered
with 'M A R I A'. See? Here
I will not cry but I tell you
every stitch was a tear.
We refuse the black mantilla
until we know. We have
asked the questions. We have
listened to the lies. Now
we write history with our feet.

This is my daughter, Maria.
Her smile is getting older.
Maybe she is getting older, too.
She is beautiful, even
in black and white. Can you
imagine her in colour?

Lydia Kennaway

Songs of Praise

A man kneels on the earth floor
and prays to Gabriel for his life.

He is on the very edge of Europe.
Once we camped there

waiting for a ferry and the kids
dug holes with seaside spades

and all night the lighthouse beam
swept our canvas house.

The interviewer asks if it is right
to try to enter a country illegally

and the student priest replies
with courtesy that it is not

but what are we supposed to do?

Carole Bromley

Flitin'

Today at the end of term service we say goodbye
to Oliver who starts a new school next term
and is very excited about his new house,
give him a round of applause,
watch the head teacher shake his small hand.

In six strange yards I wore the wrong colour,
wrong face, wrong accent. Even my words
were snatched from me and chucked
round the playground over my head:
clemmed, mardy, bairn, jammy, tarra.

I learnt to keep my gob shut till I knew
the new words, till my mum had scrimped
for the new uniform though I was allowed
to wear my good brown shoes out
among that alien sea of black leather.

Dinner was lunch now and tea was dinner
a butty was a sandwich, a bap a bread-bun
goodies were sweets and scran was grub
aye was yes and brass was money.
They laughed. I didn't find it funny.

Mash was brew and parky was cold,
there was no faffing now, no more larking
allus, summat and nowt were out
nobody offered me chuddy,
nobody gave me a croggy.

I was up-skelled, narky, vexed,
on a Scarborough warning
till I mastered this foreign tongue.
I wouldn't change places with Oliver.
Flitin'? Me? Not bloody likely. No ta.

Carole Bromley

Present

I don't ask how you came to be here,
if you're shipwrecked, on this island.

I don't ask why, or if you chose this
Yorkshire city, built on wool.

I don't ask what you've lost, or who
you may have had to leave behind.

We talk about other things:
bus routes, rain, the fractured sky.

The words pour out and I'm amazed.
You can laugh in four languages.

You tell me what you want to do,
a new script in a different place.

We gaze together at the future:
you are working, busy, proud.

Your hands are strong, palms open,
offering your unwrapped gift.

Emma Storr

Resurrection

Empty of all metaphor
Black sky
Starlight streams
Invisible pulses
From worlds
Before time

Bones in caves
Black hands on rock
Ice falling
Water rising
Icarus flying
Wings aflame

I too can rise, like a saviour
Stand tall from this wheelchair
Run across mountains
Melt into wind

What do you believe
To be gold
In all this treasure
We tiptoe through?

Eileen Neil

Coral made

Some boys are worth
saving
some boys are worth
crying for
some boys are worth
shooting dead
some boys are worth
keeping
some boys are worth
holding
their weight in gold
some boys are worth
dying for
some boys are worth
searching
some boys are worth
keeping at bay
some boys are worth
a drop in the ocean
some boys are worth
some boys are worth
loving
some boys are worth
kissing
some boys are worth
keeping at sea
some boys are worth
divers
some boys are worth
a sea change.

Rachel Bower

TV haibun

She looks suspiciously at my breasts through the screen. My own sack baby nestles on my chest; brimful of pearl. These breasts leak more milk than he could ever drink. The girl infant is still staring; it would be dangerous to meet the eyes. Dusty ribs, she is dry. Her mother's body, flat: gave everything to grow this child: nothing more to give. My folds ripple the story of his birth; provide fruit. It is too lush. She looks away, light as butterfly bones. I hoped for babbling but she is arid. It scorches there, while we eat snow. I glance at glowing logs, shift, careful not to wake him, plump and content. I wish my petals were not closed to her. *Come, gorge here. You are mine too. Ours. Come, drink, I am yours*

melting butter sun

drip light on dust, yolk on sand

syrup on dry land

Rachel Bower

Scenes from a Cold War Childhood

In the cabbage patch, there are steel mushrooms and books carved from trees, leaves that combust on contact with daylight, and small boys with branches like guns playing at war as if it wasn't happening just over the hill. Black shapes could be geese or bombers, and twigs crack like guns or bones. Tin roofs ring like steel mushrooms, trees are shaved paper-thin, skin combusts on contact with air, and small boys with guns play at death as if it wasn't happening next door. Red shapes could be fire or wounds, and the day cracks like teeth or skulls. Mushroom clouds bloom like steel and trees are shadows made of ash, roofs combust on contact with nightmares, and small boys with white paint and mushrooms for eyes play at surgeons as if steel could sew black shapes into bones and skin. In the cabbage patch, white shapes could be books or nothing.

Oz Hardwick

Desperate for a seat

After work, the walk from bus stop to platform 16
is near on impossible. Desperate in the foyer,
I ask a woman to give me her seat (there are only

five seats on the concourse, the result of a rubbish
refurbishment). I ask Customer Services if I
might get a wheelchair across the station, but

no-one is available to push. I walk unsteady with my stick.
Lucky for me, after the barriers, there are two odd benches
shoved together. This means the arm-free ends

make a glorious spread, a corner two-seater on which
I can lie down. I close my eyes, relieve my back and hip.
I may be crying. A woman asks if I am alright.

I am not alright. I am here in Leeds to work. Something
is wrong with this. I rest for 15 minutes then lurch upright,
edge towards the escalator, legs juddering. Cross the bridge,

take the lift down to my platform. I arrive at the rear
of the platform and see no seats. How sad it is that
access provisions are often placed so far away

from seats! Such access assumes ready strength,
insists we walk or roll *greater* lengths than non-disabled folk
to find the lift, the dropped kerb, the route through.

A five-minute walk has taken thirty. Thirty! I may collapse
but I've reached a seat finally, and crumple gently instead.
Really, I am always collapsing, but do so *with planning*.

This is my life now: planned collapses, 'rest' to avert more serious
disaster. This is not desirable, but who would pay me
to stay home? I wish someone would applaud my efforts

not to make a mess in public, but overall, I'd rather
a better rail service, accessible stations, a local, part-time job.
Or money to pay my bills and rest... Rest! A reckless concept.

Hereafter, I'll use a power chair, but don't expect
plain sailing from that. I have friends with wheelchairs;
I've heard the horror stories.

Cath Nichols

Why I Don't Like Wednesdays

1

I rev hopelessly on the platform: carriage entrance
and ramp too steep. Get out, switch to manual
so the guard can push my wheelchair up.
I tell him *where* to push but he does not listen
and grabs the chair the best he can and shoves.
My power chair is not designed to be pushed –
there are no handles, the seat folds down
with pressure on the back. I hear grating.
This train is too old, the guard admits, and should
be out of service, but the stock gets revived
when other engines fail. My reverse has dwindled
to next to nothing and may be damaged. I am
required to reverse into a designated
safe spot – except on this first train where there is
no designated safe spot.
The Transpennine train is safer, but still my day
compresses from hard to infinitely hard.
The narrow lift in the Parkinson building must be
entered front on and exited in reverse.
No wriggle room whatsoever. I am
eternally slow. Doors shut on me.

2

Chair is fixed! It was only the joystick
crushed into the arm restricting my reverse,
nothing major needing a spare part
(or money spent). I am lucky. Still,
unnecessary stress.
Today, my train is late arriving in Leeds
and the booked taxi did not wait.
I cried.
I have lost my phone and threw myself
on the mercy of a stranger.

3

A woman I see each Wednesday with her toddler, sighs.
'If I know you're going to be here, why don't they?'

The next train's on time; it's my taxi that's late.
He parks at an angle that does not acknowledge

this tarmaced square has kerbs. Why?
Why?! Questions involving taxis, trains, worsening

timetables, the fact I do not even qualify
for a Disabled Person's Railcard ferret through my head.

I wish there were a real, tame ferret sitting
on my lap, soft, content to be.

Stroking lowers stress, apparently.

Cath Nichols

Invisible injuries

Respecting her privacy we didn't intrude but took turns
to check the rhythm of her curtains.
My mistake was to offer a cake dusted with icing sugar.
She knocked it to the floor; shut me out.
To save face I disengaged
but Graham from the cul-de-sac
stuck two fingers up to threats of prosecution.
He broke in through her kitchen window
called the ambulance.
She came home today loaded with prescriptions
but those of us who understand the deviousness of demons
continue to monitor the rhythm of her curtains.

Sandra Burnett

"B comes to stay at my place"

B comes to stay at my place

B comes to stay at my place

Because he is waiting to move to the new place

Which is also someone else's place

Instead of his own.

I want to say no

But realise how difficult for me to do

B has nowhere to stay

Because of genuine love for blue

Blue not the colour

But the boy he loves

I feel embarrassed to know

Since I am also of colour

The colour yellow is not always helpful

To find a roof for two

B and I then become friends

Because neither of us has a home

Ann Wong

In which God appears as a busker

The stand-up comedian Tim Vine
was forced to abandon his 'Pen behind the ear' routine

after many months of practice turned him
inadvertently pro, lodged it in muscle memory,

sharpening whichever senses guarantee safe landing.
It was the punchline that killed the joke –

people will root for a blundering underdog
but not a master catcher at the top of his game.

You cite this as proof that the busker who plays the flute
near City Square, and has done for years,

is either mad or a virtuoso, peerless
in his jaunty refusal of tune

despite a lifetime of rehearsal. You hope
it's deliberate, applaud the anarchic attempt

to divert the steady ebb and flow of commuters,
to charm our lunch money from us with a yelp and a wry smile.

I have a theory that he's a prophet telling a story
with no foregone conclusion, but I don't know,

maybe it is a ruse or maybe he is simply a man
who moves to his own rhythm and asks his city to make room.

Kristina Diprose

The Truth Project

The Truth Project, as part of the Independent Inquiry into Child Sexual Abuse, receives the testimony of victims/survivors. Anonymised summaries of many people's experiences are published online.

We are writing the story of this scattered atrocity.
We detail each item of desecration
of our fond lives,
the theft

of safety, innocence, trust, spontaneity, the deaths
of so many, the utter ruin of so many.
This is spoken and counted
and stored

as we survivors unpeel the dressings from our wounds,
state times and dates and places, delineate
crimes, speak the names
of the guilty.

And look - we are myriad. We are plotting each point
on the scatter-graph, drawing the map,
building a stronghold
of fact.

We stand, stand by each other in our hurt and strength,
with the truth of what we know was done
as we piece this history
together.

Jane Kite

Stonewall

50 years on,
from a cultural revolution.
At the hands of oppression
and police brutality,
the birth of pride
allowed me to accept my sexuality.

In the UK,
because life is now better for gay men.
Pride has become a piss-up,
not a protest.
But the beneficiaries of progress
are not always progressive.

There's more to do
than rest on our laurels.
Marsha P Johnson didn't fight,
for an annual glittery parole.
Or for the scriptwriters to leave
a convenient transgender plot hole.

To misquote a famous acronym;
Ask not what your culture can do for you,
Ask what you can do for your culture.
Well...
What the fuck have we ever done?

Dusty Springfield, Elton John.
Kenneth Williams, Rock Hudson.
Oscar Wilde and EM Forster.
Billie Jean King, Patricia Routledge.
Harvey Milk and Lily Savage.
Larry Grayson, shut that door!
And to top it off,
thanks to Alan Turing
we even won the fucking war.

So, don't just put our names on the list.
Get us in VIP.
Yes, that's positive discrimination,
And as a queen,
I declare it a royal decree.

Jack Mac

Madness

If I were the man
in a black padded anorak
stiff arms
cradling hands at odd angles
down from his bent shoulders
a crooked windmill
drawing in still air

in the middle of a vast grey pavement

crowds of people skirting around him

crossing at the traffic lights
heading back to the office
turning towards Harvey Nick's
rushing for the train for a day trip to the Lake District
clearing the drains
high-tailing to burgle the house on the edge of the estate
earning £1000 an hour for a presentation

I would not be sure
of these tight-rope walkers
working hard
to avoid the cracks
walking a line
to keep their balance.

Moira Garland

The outsiders

There will always be outsiders, those who mean well, who want to help, who want to stem the swell of misery when they step into the street and see what they believe to be a tyranny of poverty.

But there's some things they don't understand, they cannot get the hang of the way things work around here – it's not clear what the rules of the game are.

They're shocked, at the grimness, at the grey, at the way people have been flayed by circumstance they see no chance of escape from this place, no trace of grace, hope displaced by inequality, that's the truth they see but folks around here would disagree you see...

They have no recognition of the badge of deprivation outsiders peering in are looking to pin on their skin, their patience is wearing thin from being called "poor" from being labelled "underprivileged."

They flinch at the blindness of the rich who only think in terms of pounds, and pence, in nice houses and picket fences and fail to see beyond the aesthetics, the crime statistics, fail to see the theme of love, belief, resilience.

A seam only seen by the keenest of the keen, they can try, but they'll always be outsiders looking in, straining eyes but they cannot see the burning rim of this kingdom; they're not in the ring.

They don't know how to sing the song, dance to the beat they've never felt the heat, felt the pressure, lived the stress, known the measure of a life where there's no plan B, no place to retreat to if things don't work out.

THIS IS NOT A ROMANTICISED DREAM!

Poverty is only romanticised by those who have never known the groan of knowing that they are alone in this shit, in a dark pit, and it's all on them to climb walls designed to keep them in line rather than giving them a leg up – the systems fucked, silver spoons don't want to touch the muck so...

Responsibility's abdicated.

Culpability's repudiated.

Liability's abdicated and life continues.... as scripted.

Becky Howcroft

Heretic

Ecce ancilla dominae
I will have on my grave,
for the mason won't know
and the parson won't notice, though
some who come by may well say
'What a quaint error!'
Of this, in my terror's my purpose today.

Anna Sutcliffe

Thomas Piketty picks his way through the shattered shopfronts

He's at a conference in Leeds
when the fighting starts.
As soon as he hears he skips the plenary
and heads for the Headrow, the Headrow aglow
with burning riot vans.

Down Briggate the plate glass tinkles
under his feet like small change,
like worthless currency. In the distance
the rattle of small-arms fire,
the tap-tap, tap-tap of Chinooks.

The mannequins eye him as he goes,
arms and legs at all angles,
their high cheekbones,
their catwalk scowls all there is
to suggest their surprise that here
among the teargas and riot gear,
here outside the chapel of Our Lady
of Teargas is Thomas Piketty,
Piketty who saw through it all,
Piketty who followed the money,
Piketty who saw it coming.

In Harvey Nicks they are lighting candles
at the altar of Our Lady of Teargas,
they are lighting candles for her children
on the streets of Athens and London,
New Orleans and Ferguson, Missouri.
Be with us now in Trafalgar and Tiananmen,
on the Champs Élysées and in Times Square,
be with us as we face the tanks and the truncheons,
the teargas and sirens, your blue

the blue of flashing lights,
the blue of the baton charge.

Piketty steps through the shattered shopfront
into the remains of the foodhall.
The makeshift congregation turns
at the crunch of the glass under his heels.
The celebrant smiles. You are just in time
she says to read us the first lesson.

Ian Harker

Come the Revolution.

Don't spend your time on earth without purpose
The addictive fiction of capitalism isn't worth it
My spirit's free in God, so we can freestyle verses
But citizens will judge you by the products you purchase

Hypodermics turning children with a shot in their arm
Light pollution fools the hooligans lost in the dark
They sing "We shall never be slaves" are you sure you aren't?
'cause a chain can be wages paying off your credit cards and overdrafts

Now even the homeless are hidden
Can you see the contraction in the "United Kingdom"?
Anonymous money's making unanimous decisions
Stealing raw materials to feed your raw materialism

Listen, let me explain the enigma
Now the only thing we demonstrate is we're ignorant
So called progress suppressed the real predicament
I look at the sky to find it's all gone digital

Fat cats withhold facts, win the rat race
But you know they're still a rat, not some kind of saint
It's like they lost their soul in a decimal place
Mistaking acquaintances for their sons and heirs, and grace is

A word with misunderstood usage
While a child is exploited a world away from which live
Apathetic to the truth of what the future is
Are we connected to the truth of what the future is?

We got a 'third world' mentality in a 'first world' state
We got time on our hands, it leaves a blood red stain
Scott-Heron told the truth about the home and the hate
Revolutionaries asking: "Can we spare some change?"

It's all fair game with no political thought
People get bought like the media get paid to distort
Scapegoat asylum seekers and claim there's no justice
People want an opinion but only online they'll discuss it

There's nothing I can do except rhyme and reason
It's all globalised, both the good and the evil
We got a choice to make and we got music inside us
The revolution has died.

That's why I'm speaking in the one-minute silence

Testament